Strathclyde Open Rope Exchange

Showing you the ropes since 2014

Basic Rope Safety

&

Emergencies Management

CONTENTS:

Introduction & Background

What is STORE?

The Strathclyde Open Rope Exchange is pretty much what it says on the tin: a regular meeting in the Strathclyde area which is open to all people interested in rope, rope art and rope bondage.

Who is STORE for?

Anyone interested in rope regardless of experience level, style or role. You can learn to tie, come and be tied, share your knowledge or simply observe. You can participate as much or as little as you like.

Why was STORE started?

Scotland, particularly Central Scotland, has a rapidly expanding group of rope practitioners from various styles, philosophies and approaches. There are regular Peer Workshops and individual tuition opportunities along with regular club nights (Rebound and Club T) that provide dedicated space and experienced attendees in a multitude of styles. STORE is intended to compliment the already available resources whilst adding a different flavour by holding themed educational events on a semi-regular basis.

Where will it be held?

At the moment the plan is to hold semi-regular events at the premises of Club Rebound. Additional venues are also being considered to hold events.

How much will it cost?

As much as hiring the venue costs split across the number of people attending. STORE is a non-profit venture and many of the workshops are offered in return for voluntary donations.

CHAPTER 1: SAFETY EQUIPMENT YOU SHOULD OWN

Being safe starts with having the right tools and knowledge to respond to a situation gone wrong. Below we'll describe a few items that we think are essential to the well prepared kit bag along with the pros and cons of each choice.

All the described items can be found for sale in the STORE Amazon Shop

SAFETY SHEARS AND LINE CUTTERS

Before you consider tying someone up, or getting tied up yourself, you should give serious thought to how you will remove the rope in an emergency. What kind of emergencies? Rope may be cutting off circulation to a limb, causing excessive pain or have slipped to a dangerous position. The person being tied may suddenly take unwell. The person doing the tying could become incapacitated also. There could be a fire or another sudden event requiring quick release. Basically you will need a quick, effective and safe method for removing rope.

EMT Shears

EMT Shears are basic, simple, heavy duty scissors. Paramedics and other healthcare professionals have been using these for years. They can cut through most materials including ropes (both loose and under tension) but pose very little risk to the user or person within the ropes. At under £2 a pair they can almost be considered

disposable. No tears would be shed if you lost your shears rather than your expensive rescue knife and you can push the boat out and buy several pairs and leave them in multiple places. Take care to only buy recognised brands such as Steroplast's TufKuts. Saving 50p by buying a cheap knock off that doesn't actually do the job is not a saving at all.

Rescue hooks

These dedicated tools are designed to be quickly deployed and used with one hand while posing minimal risk to oneself or other people. Some care is needed not to catch your fingers in the line of cutting. Like all tools with a specific function they are fairly specialised and so do not necessarily replace the need for shears but can be used in addition. As with safety shears there are no issues with carrying a rescue hook in public places.The Gerber Hook pictured costs £20 and takes standard Stanley blades. It is the most pricey of all the options listed, but probably the longest lasting.It is also the tool of choice for many paramedics and armed forces personnell. Unfortunately they are becoming harder to obtain as Gerber has ceased production.

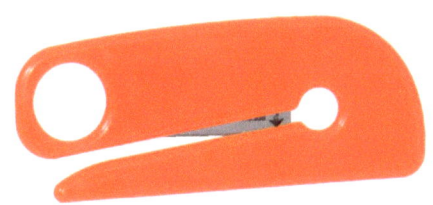

If you can't get hold of the Gerber Hook then this Line Cutter also comes highly recommended and will handle cutting through just about any thickness of rope with ease. The blade can be re-sharpened and it comes in at around £18.

The only truly evidence based cutters are those recommended by NHS services in the UK for the removal of ligatures in the context of self strangulation and self harm. These hooks are the Res-Q hook and the Barrington LC1 which are named as approved devices in multiple NHS Trust's policies. They are however more expensive and they are required to cut much tougher materials than rope in order to be considered effective.

Seatbelt cutters

A good halfway house between shears and a rescue hook and as the name suggests are originally designed to cut seatbelts in an emergency. It is almost impossible to cut yourself by accident (please don't try prove us wrong!) and they will cut through *most* ropes in a flash. We wouldn't however be confident in using them as a first line for ropes >6mm diameter. They do however make a great kit bag addition as a backup.

The blades are non-replaceable and non-sharpening. Each cutter costs about £3.

Rescue knives

In short, we don't recommend using these for rope work. They are of course very effective, but many are not legal to be carried in the UK due to weapons laws and they are very easy to use in a way that causes injury, especially if someone is in a panic.

First Aid Kits & Aftercare

A general First Aid Kit is always useful. The injuries likely to be sustained during rope practice are similar in many ways to general sports injuries, so a sports kit is probably a very useful thing to have. We've also found this kit online that is described as a motorist's kit which has everything you need. If you ask in advance there are STORE first aid kits available for £10 also. In addition to the standard items we would recommend that all kits have instant ice packs to treat potential joint or nerve injuries, a bottle of water and a bar of chocolate which work wonders for "feeling a bit odd" and a little tub of Sudocream in case of rope burns.

CHAPTER 2: Things You Should Know About Your Partner's Health and Wellbeing

It is important to know your partner a little before doing rope together, but there's a huge difference between what you need to know and violating personal boundaries. A partner is not obliged to tell you their life story or disclose all of their medical history, but they should be able to give you the following information to allow you to assess whether it is safe to proceed or not.

Questions to the person being tied:

Mobility

Sounds obvious, doesn't it? Knowing the physical limitations of your partner is important, so find out as much as you can before you run into trouble.

> *Do you have any problems with your joints or flexibility?*
> *Do you have any old injuries that might be a problem?*
> *Are there any positions you find difficult?*

If you plan to do a tie that requires flexibility the receiving partner should try hold the position without ropes first to assess how long they are likely to be able to hold it.

Circulation

There is a range of normal when it comes to circulation in the limbs, so find out what is normal for yourself or your partner?

> *Do you have any problems with your hands or feet getting cold normally?*
> *Have you had any problems with your circulation before?*

It can be a good idea to feel the temperature of the hands and feet before starting so that a better assessment of circulation can be carried out later. Oddly enough someone with cold feet normally will still have cold feet when tied up!

Fits and Funny turns

This can be quite a sensitive topic, but if you don't ask then you don't know for sure. It can be fine to tie someone with a history of seizures if you get to know them and their warning signs. If in doubt it's ok to say that you're not sure if it is safe to continue.

> *Have you ever had a fit or funny turn when being tied? Can you tell me a bit about it?*
> *Have you had one recently?*
> *Are you able to predict when they happen?*
> *What is helpful to do if it happens?*
> *Can you still use your safe word/signal at these times?*

Mental Health and Psychological Issues

Again, this is a bit of a difficult subject for some, but you really are better off asking some general questions just in case. It is perfectly ok to say that you don't need to know lots of details and indeed that might be reassuring to some people that you don't want to pry but want to be prepared.

> *Are there any issues with your emotional and psychological response to being tied that I should know about?*
> *Are there particular situations, actions or words that should be avoided during tying?*
> *Should I be worried if you cry?*

Don't pressure someone into giving you detail if they seem reluctant. People with mental health and trauma issues are more than capable of engaging in safe, sane and consensual situations and are usually the best person to make the judgement about whether it is safe to continue. People can also laugh or cry, become loud or silent or any other behavioural response and it can be quite normal for them. It can be disconcerting to have someone break into floods of tears if you haven't asked about it beforehand.

Sensory issues

Some people have sensory issues you need to know about. This can be lack of sensation or hypersensitivity to sensation. If someone may be unable to hear or see you during a tie it is important to know. Someone with sensorial issues will appreciate you thinking to ask about it?

> *Do you have any problems with your hearing or vision?*
> *Do you have any problems with sensitivity to touch?*
> *Do you have any areas of numbness or reduced sensitivity?*
> *How do you feel about deliberate sensory manipulation? (ie blindfolds, strenuous positioning etc)*

QUESTIONS TO THE PERSON DOING THE TYING.

A lot of focus is put on assessing the person being tied in relation to fitness, but it is extremely important that the person who is doing the tying is subject to the same kind of checks. Many of the above questions apply equally in this case, but here's a few more things to consider asking.

Are there any physical or emotional issues affecting your tying just now?
Do you have any health problems that may affect your ability to respond quickly in an emergency?
Do you need to wear glasses or a hearing aid? If yes, do you have it with you?
If I fall or collapse will you be able to support my weight?
If you suddenly take unwell and are unable to untie me, how do I get free?

The last question is highlighted here as it is a situation that few people prepare for. At a workshop or event there are lots of people around who can step in, but if you are working alone together then this question should be seriously considered.

Chapter 3: Setting Up a Safe Rope Environment

Checking Your Equipment

This should be obvious, but the most important thing you can do to increase the safety of your equipment is to check it over before you plan to use it.

- Locate your cutting device and check that it is sharp
- Locate your backup cutting device and check that it is sharp
- Check over the rope you plan to use for damage and replace if necessary
- Check your accessory equipment for damage (rings, carabiners, straps etc)

Setting the Room

Obviously tying in a well set up room is better than just starting to tie without checking

- Is the floor clear of trip & fall hazards such as hard corners of furniture?
- Is the room warm/cool enough?
- Have you checked for things that may catch on a moving rope?
- Is your equipment in an easy to access place?
- Are observers far enough back from your tieing space?
- If you are using someone else's suspension point have you satisfied yourself that it is safe and fit for purpose? It is YOUR responsibility to check this.

It is often the case that people forget about good etiquette when watching someone tie. They'll try to catch your attention, ask questions or even possibly come into your space while you are working. Politely but firmly tell them to wait until later. Have a think about what you will say beforehand.

Safe Words, Safe Signs & Checking In

It can be very useful to develop a language with your partner for how to communicate when problems are arising. Within STORE we aim to develop a common language for everyone to use. Make sure if you are setting up signs and words that both of you know exactly what they mean.

Safe words

We prefer the classic RED, AMBER and GREEN

- RED means stop immediately and release all bindings.
- AMBER means a problem is developing which needs discussed
- GREEN means all is ok

It can be incredibly useful if safe words are used along with extra information to guide how the person in control of the rope should react. For example:

- "RED OUT NOW"means the rope needs to come off immediately (if no qualifier is given then this is the standard meaning of RED used alone)
- "RED 5 mins" means "I need to be untied but I think you have 5 mins to do so" which is helpful for situations that are becoming intolerable but are not yet an emergency. People with experience in being tied are often very good judges of their abilities.
- "AMBER left arm numb" means "my left arm has gone numb so something needs fixed"
- "AMBER leg rope slipping" points out a rope that has moved

Always beware of the person who goes silent when they relax into their rope headspace. Many people describe losing the ability to talk in this state.

Safe signs

Lots of people prefer non-verbal communication where possible with rope. To do this safely you need ways of checking that everything is ok. We suggest the following:

- Tapping a hand against the floor or body means whatever is happening right now is too difficult or painful and must stop immediately
- Shaking the head means stop and check what is wrong
- If the rigger squeezes the hand of the person being tied they are asking for a return squeeze to confirm all is ok
- If the rigger places their hand firmly on the shoulder they are asking for a nod or shake of the head to confirm all is ok

If working in an environment that is dimly lit (as many clubs and venues are) it may be best to agree to use verbal signs in preference. We've also seen people use bells attached to the tied partner's wrist or having them hold an object that they will drop if there is a problem.

No matter which method is used the person being tied has the last say.
Stop means stop.

Checking in

Aside from the above it is important for the person doing the tying to check regularly for common problems such as pressure, circulation and nerve issues. Some may not even be noticed by the person being tied unless checked. A good routine would be:

- Check the temperature of the extremities (hands and feet) for changes. Remember you'll need to know if your partner naturally has cold hands or feet for this to be useful!
- Check the skin for discolouration. Reduced circulation makes skin appear red, blue, purple or even white. This is really easy to check on caucasian skin but harder on darker skin tones. Check the capillary return by pressing hard against a bony area and count how long it takes for the skin to return to normal colour. If this takes longer than 3 seconds there is restricted circulation which needs attention

- Hand squeezes can be used to assess potential nerve issues due to ropes on the upper arm but are not comprehensive. If there is any reduced strength noted the ropes need to come off immediately.
- A better test for nerve issues in the upper limb is to ask the subject to flex and extend their wrist. This is much better assessment of the radial nerve. If the subject is unable to do this motion the rope needs to come off immediately.

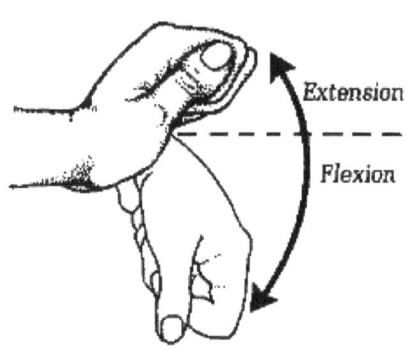

- Hand squeezes or verbal questioning can assess the conscious level of a partner. Some people seem quieter or less responsive when being tied so it's good practice to check things are ok. If you are in doubt about the ability of the person to communicate with you stop and assess the situation

Aftercare & Tidying up

After a rope session both the person being tied and the one doing the tying need a bit of time and space to ground themselves. Plan for this in advance.

- Keep a bottle of water or two on hand. It's amazing how much of a sweat and thirst you can build up doing rope.
- Body temperature often drops at the end of any physical activity. Have a warm blanket, jumper or other clothing on hand.
- Some people benefit from having a quick snack after doing rope. Good things to have on hand are cereal bars and chocolate.
- Agree beforehand what you both need. Some people like to be alone for a while, or go to a quiet place to sit. Knowing exactly what you need to do makes the whole process go smoothly. It is likely that people will want to come up to you to say something about your tie and forget to wait until you are ready. Have a plan in mind for how to deal with this.
- When tying in a public venue it is good manners to gather up your rope and vacate the tying space for others to use as soon as you can.
- Due to the nature of tying and the physical activity it entails there may be ropes that will need washed afterwards. A good idea is to coil these ropes differently from the others so you can identify them later.
- Aim to leave the space as you found it. Obviously in your own home you set your own rules!

Chapter 4: Common Problems Encountered During Rope Bondage

Marks, Bruising & Rope Burns

Rope marks, indentations on the skin in the shape of the rope, are pretty much standard issue when it comes to most ties. Generally they will fade over the following few hours.

There are marks that look like thin lines or little spots that happen in between ropes in wraps. You can limit these occurring by carefully dressing your ropes during the tie (run two fingers under the rope to re-lay them evenly and without skin caught between them). These marks tend to last a couple of days and need no specific treatment.

Bruising can occur where areas of high pressure occur or where there has been restricted circulation which makes bruising more likely in response to even minor injury. In most cases this is self-limiting and will resolve over the next few days. Many people find bruising reduces faster using arnica tincture on the affected area.

Rope burns happen when rope passes over the skin at a high enough speed to generate friction and heat. This is more common with synthetic fibre ropes. Keeping the affected area clean is usually enough to remedy it. Application of an antiseptic healing cream such as Sudocrem can help the healing along. Bear in mind that if a rope has caused a friction burn that it has broken the skin and the rope has potentially been in contact with body fluids. The affected rope should be washed or otherwise treated.

Circulation Issues vs Nerve Damage

There is a separate STORE session on the anatomy and neurology of the upper and lower limb that will cover this topic in more detail. Check the website for more details.

Telling the difference between the numbness and tingling that happens due to reduced circulation versus that caused by nerve compression is quite a difficult topic to convey by words alone. There is no 100% foolproof method of detecting the difference in practice, but certain signs and symptoms are good to know about.

People with experience of being tied, particularly in suspensions, can often tell the difference between "good pain" and "bad pain". As with all other issues regarding the subjective experience of the person being tied their opinion trumps that of the person doing the tying.

<u>Nerve damage can occur in seconds</u> and take months to resolve. In some cases the nerve damage is permanent. It is better to untie and tie again than persevere with a tie that is causing issues.

As a general rule of thumb avoid placing ropes within 5-7cm (three fingers' width) of a joint. Take care with any rope that passes through the armpit.

<u>Characteristics of circulation-type issues:</u>
- The skin is discoloured.
- There is numbness or tingling in the whole limb or whole hand/foot
- Capillary return is reduced
- The limb is cold to the touch
- Movement remains normal until it becomes severe

<u>Characteristics of nerve-type issues:</u>
- The pain is of a burning or "electric shock" type
- Numbness and tingling occurs in specific areas only
- The subject cannot flex and extend their wrist
- There is loss of power or movement in the hand/foot
- In certain cases there is a drop in blood pressure causing dizziness, nausea and possible fainting.

If "electric shock" or sharp pains occur stop and untie immediately. This is almost certainly nerve pain.

Mental & Emotional First Aid
Sometimes people have very emotional reactions to being tied which can either be a very positive experience or unfortunately a negative one. Knowing what to do should you or your partner experience this makes it much less traumatic all round.

Sudden inexplicable crying
Some people experience this regularly when being tied and others never at all. It is confusing and a little frightening. In this situation we presume the person has no immediate explanation of how they are feeling.

What to do: Offer reassurance. And tissues. Let them know that lots of people experience this and it is normal. It most certainly does not mean there is anything wrong with the person!

Reminder of a traumatic event

Unfortunately some people have had bad experiences where they felt out of control or unable to escape. Many go on to have wonderful experience with rope, but a few carry painful memories with them that may be reactivated by being bound. The important thing to remember is to stay calm and don't take it personally.

What to do: Gently and quietly remove the rope. Tell your partner that they are safe and you are letting them out. They may feel they are disappointing you, and they may not believe you that they are not. Let them know you can always tie again in a while. Don't ask prying questions. "Talking it out" is rarely useful whilst emotions are hot. You do not need to know the details. It is enough to acknowledge your partner is distressed and you are not angry or upset by that. If someone wants to elaborate on the details on what has happened to them in the past simply listen. Don't use phrases like "don't be silly" or anything else that minimises their experience. You're not a therapist or an investigator, so keep your replies supportive and non-challenging. If there is a major issue that needs dealt with then the time to do that is when the person is calm and there is an experienced clinician available. You can re-traumatise someone making them give details and make things a lot worse than they are. The majority of people with traumatic experiences never go through professional therapy, and many of them are just fine.

Alcohol & Drugs

 In short, intoxication with any substance should mean no rope happens at all. No exceptions. Don't feel pressured into working with someone who is intoxicated. All accidents and injuries are more likely in the presence of alcohol and drugs.

Chapter 5: Practical Management of Emergencies

Cutting the rope vs untying

It is difficult to cover in writing which situations are best to cut the rope and which to untie. Both approaches can be the right thing to do. Cutting through ropes that are helping to hold a person's weight can cause injury during a fall, but equally not cutting the rope may be causing a potentially life threatening situation. Untying the lines may be more appropriate, especially if the person has not yet come to any harm and a more controlled approach will be safer.

If in doubt, support the person's weight and cut the ropes. Rope is replaceable. People are not.

Safe removal of tight bindings

A ligature cutter is most effective when used to cut softer and thinner materials but will also cut tougher materials, but more effort may be required and the cutting process may take longer. Avoid cutting through any knots, as it makes a removal attempt more difficult owing to multiple layers at the point of the knot.

When cutting a line that is under load, such as suspension lines, you should be prepared to take the weight off the load immediately. Don't let a bound person fall to the floor as they are unable to protect themselves from injury.

To optimise the use of the ligature cutter, the rounded and blunt end should be initially placed flat against the person's body so that it can slide under the ligature. Once the ligature cutter has been located between the person's body and the ligature, the ligature cutter should be turned so that the sharp edge of blade faces the ligature i.e. with the opening away from the person. Pull away from the person's body, using a rocking or sawing motion, so that the ligature cutter cuts through the ligature material.

In situations where the person resists actions to remove the ligature, it may be appropriate to restrict the person's ability to struggle, especially where the struggling behaviour increases the risk(s) presented by the ligature, or by the use of the ligature cutter.

Once a ligature cutter has been used it should be cleaned and re-sharpened by either replacing the blade or by following the manufacturer's instructions. Some manufacturers offer a sharpening service. If there has been accidental contamination with blood this should be cleaned off with isopropyl alcohol (available at chemists either as liquid or wipes). If you have come into contact with someone else's blood you should seek medical advice regarding testing for blood borne viruses.

Practical Management of Panic

A panic attack occurs when the body experiences a rush of intense psychological (mental) and physical symptoms.

- A feeling of intense anxiety/fear/"impending doom"
- nausea
- sweating
- trembling
- a sensation that your heart is beating irregularly (palpitations)

Panic attacks can be very frightening and intense, but they are not dangerous. A panic attack will not cause you any physical harm and it is unlikely that you will be admitted to hospital if you have had a panic attack.

In the main the self -management of panic is down to the person, but knowing a bit about what helps will let you give helpful advice. "Just calm down" is not good advice!

Focus

During a panic attack, remind the person that the frightening thoughts and sensations are a sign of panic and will eventually pass. During a panic attack it is important to focus on something that is non-threatening and visible, such as the time passing on your watch, or count the tiles on the ceiling.

Slow deep breathing

While you are having a panic attack, try to focus on your breathing. Your feelings of panic and anxiety can get worse if you breathe too quickly. Try to focus on slow deep breathing while counting slowly to three on each breath in and out.

Creative visualisation

During a panic attack, lots of things can go through your mind. Some people think about disaster, or even death. Instead of letting your imagination focus on these negative thoughts, try to concentrate on positive images. Think of a place or a situation that makes you feel peaceful, relaxed or at ease. Once you know have this image in your mind, try to focus your attention on it. It should help to distract you from the situation, and it may also help ease your symptoms.

Do not fight an attack

Fighting a panic attack can often make the experience worse. Trying to resist the attack and finding that you are unable to can increase your sense of anxiety and panic. Instead, during a panic attack, reassure yourself by accepting that although it may seem embarrassing, and your symptoms may be difficult to deal with, your attack is not life-threatening. Focus on the fact that your attack will have an end and try your best to let it pass.

For excellent (and free) education about Panic Attacks and Panic Disorder by Dr Chris Williams follow this link.

HEAT INJURY & HEATSTROKE

What is a heat injury?

A loss of water and salt through sweating that causes dehydration to the body. This is particularly troublesome in hot buildings with poor ventilation. It is also applicable to people who do their rope wearing restrictive clothing or who engage in long sessions (>1hr duration)

Heatstroke is caused by prolonged exposure to high temperatures or by doing physical activity in hot weather. You are considered to have heatstroke when your body temperature reaches 40°C or higher. High humidity, certain health problems and some medications increase your risk of heatstroke. Heatstroke is the progression of two worsening heat-related conditions. When your body overheats, you first may develop heat cramps. If you don't cool down, you may progress to symptoms of heat exhaustion, such as heavy sweating, nausea, lightheadedness and feeling faint.

Heatstroke occurs if your body temperature continues to rise. At this point, emergency treatment is needed. In a period of hours, untreated heatstroke can cause damage to your brain, heart, kidneys and muscles. These injuries get worse the longer treatment is delayed, increasing your risk of serious complications or death.

Mostly this can be avoided through ensuring that everyone has had enough to drink and adding ventilation where applicable. If it is a particularly hot or humid day consider whether or not it is sensible to continue with your plan to tie.

What are the signs and symptoms of heat exhaustion?
1. Excessive sweating with pale, moist, cool skin
2. Headache
3. Weakness
4. Dizziness
5. Loss of appetite
6. Stomach cramps
7. Nausea (with or without vomiting)
8. Urge to defecate
9. Chills (Gooseflesh)
10. Rapid Breathing
11. Tingling of Hands/Feet
12. Confusion

What would the treatment be for heat exhaustion?
1. Reduce the temperature: open a window, move to another room
2. Loosen clothing
3. Apply a wet cold towel or ice pack to the forehead, neck, armpits and groin
4. Drink small amounts of cold water to rehydrate: don't drink large volumes quickly
5. Elevate the legs above the level of the heart
6. If symptoms do not resolve with basic measures seek medical help
7. Even if symptoms resolve do not do further physical activity in the same day

What are the signs and symptoms of heat stroke?
1. Skin is red, hot and dry
2. Weakness
3. Dizziness
4. Confusion
5. Headaches
6. Seizures
7. Nausea
8. Stomach pains or cramps
9. Respiration and pulse may be rapid and weak.
10. Unconsciousness and collapse may occur suddenly.

What would the treatment be for heat stroke?

As for heat exhaustion except in this instance you MUST seek medical attention. This is a medical emergency.

Loss of consciousness

If your partner loses consciousness for more than a few seconds for any reason you must seek medical help. Being unconscious means that the person is not moving and not responding to you speaking to them or to shaking them.

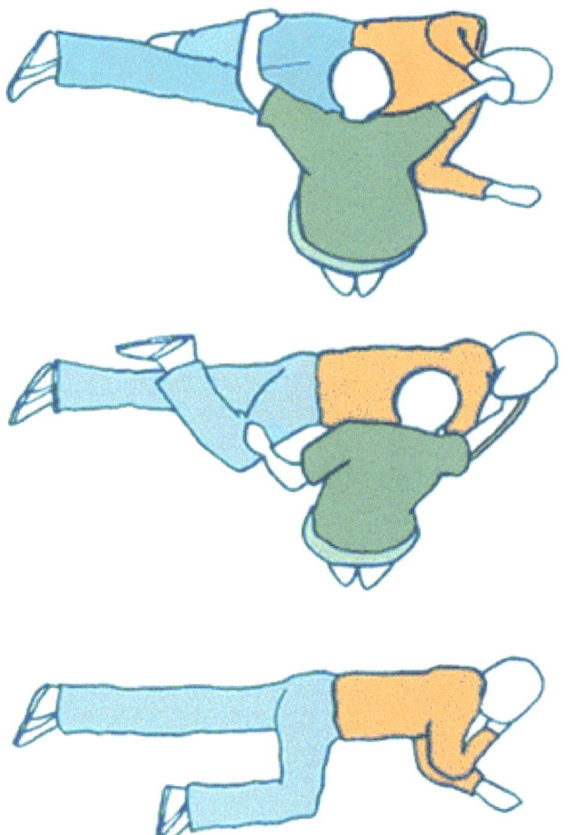

If the person is unconscious but breathing normally you will need to put them in the recovery position. Kneel next to them and bend the furthest away knee and furthest away arm as in the diagram opposite. By pulling gently towards you the person will move into the recovery position.

Stay with the casualty until help arrives, but you may have to leave to phone for an ambulance. Make sure that the casualty is still breathing and watch for any vomitting.

Seizures

You may find yourself working with someone with epilepsy or non-epileptic seizures. If a seizure occurs the important thing is to remain calm. Remove anything that may cause injury (this includes ropes!). Do NOT put anything in the casualty's mouth. You are more likely to cause a blockage of the airways than you are to prevent them biting their tongue.

After a seizure most people are tired, confused or may act a bit strangely. Try to keep them in a quiet environment and relaxed. People with seizures can lose control of their bladder or bowel during the event and may be incredibly embarrassed about this. It is ok to ask if this has happened before and what you can do to help.

Ideally you should already know where any rescue medications etc are because you will have covered the fact that the person has a seizure disorder in your negotiations. Some people with seizures don't need to go to hospital every time they have one. If however the person normally has well controlled seizures or this is a new symptom then medical help is needed.

THE NON-BREATHING COLLAPSED PARTNER

IF YOUR PARTNER IS NOT RESPONDING AND IS NOT BREATHING PHONE 999 IMMEDIATELY!!

Around 60 thousand cardiopulmonary arrests (the heart stops beating and the person stops breathing) occur outside of hospital every year in the UK[1]. Only 30 thousand of these are treated by the emergency services[2]. By far and away the most common causes of cardiorespiratory arrest in adults are fatal arrhythmias (abnormal heart beat) and this will only be "fixed" by a defibrillator or drugs. The likelihood of survival of the victim drops 10% with each passing minute until a fully trained resuscitation crew arrives. CPR, or CardioPulmonary Resuscitation to give it the proper name, given by bystanders will help improve the chances of survival. Survival until discharge from hospital varies between 2-12% of cases[3] which is only 1 in 10 people. It is highly unlikely that you will revive an arrest victim, but you might buy them enough time to get the treatment that will save them. There are however occasionally success stories from CPR only[4].

Now, we have to be very clear for this next section that **this is general, lay person advice and in no way constitutes formal training in resuscitation, first aid or any form of life support.** We recommend that all adults should consider getting themselves into a First Aid[5] or Heartstart[6] course for not just rope, but for the sake of their family and friends. Anyone who has attended a formal course will have been taught a different algorithm for life support and they should follow that instead. This advice does not supercede formal training in any way.

Is it safe to approach?

Chances are you will have been present at the moment the person lost consciousness and will have a good idea of what has happened. You should always consider your own safety first however. To give examples (all hopefully never to happen!) could the person have been electrocuted and still in contact with the electrical source? Was there a structural collapse that remains unstable? An injured rescuer only makes the victim's situation worse.

---

[1] Ambulance Service Association. National Cardiac Arrest Audit Report; 2006.

[2] Pell JP,et al Presentation, management, and outcome of out of hospital cardiopulmonary arrest: comparison by underlying aetiology. Heart 2003;89:839-42.

[3] Perkins GD, Cooke MW. Variability in cardiac arrest survival: the NHS Ambulance Service Quality Indicators.Emerg Med J 2012 29

[4] See http://www.heart.org/

[5] Courses available at http://www.redcrossfirstaidtraining.co.uk/

[6] See http://www.bhf.org.uk/heart-health/how-we-can-help/training/heartstart-training.aspx

There is no question about it at all if the person is still bound they should be cut free immediately. You will want the person to be on their back on the ground ideally.

If it is safe to do so, continue.

Is the person responding?

Give them a good shake and in a raised voice ask if they are ok. If yes, simply ask what was wrong and use common sense as to whether further assessment is needed. See above section on faints and fits.

If there is no response, continue......

Shout loudly for help and call 999

You need help and you need it fast. Let others around know you need help and either call 999 yourself or get someone else to do it for you. Ask for the Ambulance service when asked which service you require. An operator will ask you some questions. Answer them as calmly as you can.

You need to be able to tell the call handler exactly where you are, who you are & who the patient is. You need to give the person's condition first before any explanation of how it happened as this will decide how urgently the call is handled. In this instance use the phrase "collapsed and unresponsive" when describing what has happened to the victim to quickly communicate the level of urgency. Recruit others around you (if applicable) to take responsibility for going to meet the ambulance crew and guide them to you when they arrive.
An example would be:

> "My name is Jane Smith and I am at 42 West Street, Glasgow. I am with a man in his 30s who has collapsed and is not responding. He collapsed a few minutes ago and doesn't appear to be breathing."

That small amount of information is enough for the dispatcher to know you have a life threatening emergency that needs immediate response.

If you are on your own you might want to stick the phone on speakerphone so you can continue to talk to the operator. In the UK the operator stays on the line until the paramedics arrive and chances are they will talk you through the next stages.

If someone else has called for help, don't hang around listening in on the call and continue....

Do your ABCs
Airway

If someone's airway is blocked, it won't matter if their heart is still beating. They'll asphyxiate shortly. Clearing the airway is the first priority. Place your hand on their forehead and gently tilt the head back. With your fingertips under the point of the victim's chin, lift the chin to open the airway. See the section on managing choking also for more advice.

If the airway is clear, continue...

Breathing

If someone is not breathing it doesn't matter if they have a pulse or not. They'll start running out of oxygen pretty quickly. Look, Listen and Feel for breathing. Look at the chest for movement, Listen at the mouth for breath sounds, Feel with your cheek for air movement. Do this no more than 10 secs. Gasping or sighing noises do not count as normal breathing.

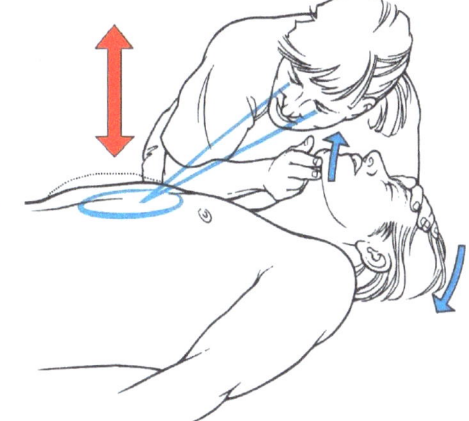

If breathing is not present or not normal, continue....

Circulation

If you've got this far then you are dealing with a cardiorespiratory arrest. Checking for a pulse wastes valuable time, and as above if the person isn't breathing then they won't have a pulse for very long. You need to commence CPR. It has been proven that lay people are notoriously bad at finding a pulse even on a live person.

At this point we will describe Hands Only CPR. If you are trained in any other variant of CPR please ignore this section. Use the algorithm for those with a duty of care or whichever is appropriate to your level of training.

HANDS ONLY CPR: HARD & FAST

Hands Only CPR is a new approach developed by the British Heart Foundation[7] for use by lay persons without formal training. The emphasis is on keeping compressions going without interruption. There are no rescue breaths given in this style.

The correct place to put your hands is in the centre of the breast bone. It doesn't have to be exact. Interlock your hands one on top of the other, palms down and press with the heel of the bottom hand.

When giving compressions ignore what you have seen in just about every movie and TV resus scene[8]. Keep your arms straight and do not bend the elbows. The thrust comes from the shoulders and hips and should compress the chest at least 6 cm (2 inches). Don't worry about breaking ribs. Better having a broken rib than being dead.

Push hard and fast at a rate of 100 compressions a minute. This is very tiring. If other people are present take turns to do the compressions. 100 beats per minute is the same as the beat of the Bee Gees' Stayin' Alive.

Do not stop unless the person wakes up or you are asked to by a paramedic.

Need a simpler way to remember all of that?

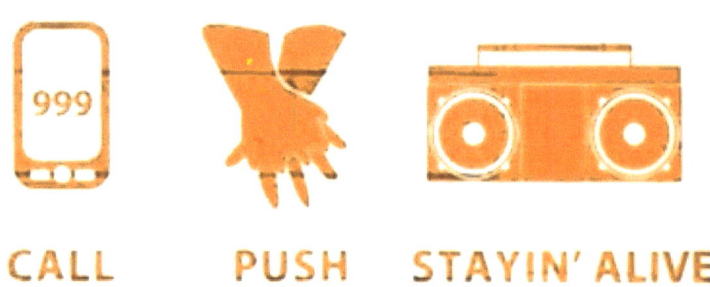

CALL   PUSH   STAYIN' ALIVE

Dial 999, push hard and fast in the centre of the chest to the beat of Stayin' Alive

Or watch the British Heart Foundation's video featuring Vinnie Jones

---

[7] http://www.bhf.org.uk/heart-health/life-saving-skills/hands-only-cpr.aspx or search for the term "Hands Only CPR"

[8] Television and movies have to pretend to give chest compressions on real people. If you actually did a chest compression on a conscious person it would be very painful indeed.

BIBLIOGRAPHY & RESOURCES

Smith, J. (Ed). Handling of People. 6th Edition. Back Care.

HSE. Manual Handling Operations Regulations 1992. HMSO.

Resuscitation Council UK. Advanced Life Support Manual. 6th Edn

Worcestershire Mental Health Partnership NHS Trust. Ligature Cutter Guidelines.

http://www.bhf.org.uk/heart-health/life-saving-skills/hands-only-cpr.aspx

Oxford Handbook of Emergency Medicine (4 ed.)
Jonathan P. Wyatt, Robin N. Illingworth, Colin A. Graham, and Kerstin Hogg

Rope Incident Reports group on Fetlife

Panic Attacks and Panic Disorder by Dr Chris Williams follow this link.

St John's Ambulance First Aid Manual, 10th Ed

www.ingramcontent.com/pod-product-compliance
Lightning Source LLC
Chambersburg PA
CBHW041831280526
45792CB00006B/2048